THE BIRDHOUSE PROJECT
COLLABORATION OF THE HEART, MIND AND HANDS

STORY AND CONCEPT BY KRIS G. MUNSCH
WRITTEN AND EDITED BY JEFF FOUQUET

COVER ART BY SHANON FOUQUET
WWW.FOOKADESIGNS.COM

The Birdhouse Project is dedicated to anyone who took the time to listen and encourage me to write this book. What started out as an idea has turned into something that will help those who have endured tragedy in their lives. Tragedy changes lives in ways you will never know unless you have experienced it for yourself. Words do not explain the depth of change you go through in these situations. That transformation can (and will) leave most people lost and waiting for direction. The idea behind this project is not to create a solid path back to civilization, but to provide a compass so that you can find some direction. I spent years living in a dark, twisted forest of loss, surrounded by many paths I considered following, but I didn't realize the compass was in my pocket the whole time.

My story is much like everyone else's who has experienced loss. We have walked that walk, but in completely different shoes. We all end up in dark, twisted forests that have a criss-crossed canopy of entanglements imprisoning us where we are. We can only stay there for so long before our bodies will start to ache for sunlight again. My path back into the light may be very different than yours, but the key is finding a path. In my experience, I found the direction I needed could be found through following the simple steps of building a birdhouse.

So I offer you a few pieces of wood and a story of survival. In the chapters ahead, I share with you my heart-felt emotions because I want you to believe that if you pick up your parts and listen to my story, you can follow these steps, put your life back together, and find yourself in a brand new place. You can do and say great things if you harness the powerful emotions within and transform them into action.

I owe many people for helping me turn this belief into action. Thank you, Gena, Jacob and the rest of my family for enduring this trip out of the forest with me. Jeff Fouquet, for your skill in guiding this project, I will be forever grateful. To the students at Bonner Springs High School, you saved my life. To anyone who has taken time out of their lives to listen to me talk about my idea that a birdhouse could possibly give people hope, I thank you. Your generous ears and kind words were the fuel that drove my passion to do and say great things for those who are still struggling in the darkness.

Blake Christopher Munsch 5/21/89 - 12/23/05

The inspiration behind this journey came from the loss of my son, Blake Christopher Munsch, on December 23rd, 2005. The sights and sounds of that night will be forever etched in many memories. The smile of a boy and the strength of his hug were gone as quickly as the wind blows past your face on a cool, sunny morning. Blake was like most sixteen year olds. He dreamed of tomorrow and rarely looked back at his footsteps. He lived with little thought of who was who or why they did the things they did. Blake was just a simple kid living every moment in the world around him.

The pictures on this page are treasured memories of a time that is in the past, but each picture is also a moment of time that lives into the future. In Blake's first sixteen years of life I tried to teach him things that I felt were tools he needed to survive. Sometimes I failed (like many parents), but I do think I had moments of success, too. My last moment with my son on this earth was of him giving me a huge hug that I can still feel when I sit quietly and revisit the moment. What he and I did not realize that day was that his grip would change lives in ways we never dreamed.

After losing Blake, I came to realize that the life lessons I thought I was teaching him would transform into the life lessons he would teach me. Blake lives on in the lives of many people I teach in high school. Every student of mine knows his story and it is my hope that some of them think of him as they face life's obstacles. His first sixteen years of life were so innocent, as if he realized the journey had just begun. I look forward to the lessons his short life has yet to teach me – today, tomorrow, forever. I love and miss you, son.

1. A NORMAL DAY

As a new woodworking instructor at an eastern Kansas high school, I took one of my classes to an all-school assembly today. The speaker was a young, male friend of one of the kids killed in the Columbine tragedy in Colorado during the late 90's. The assembly presented stories about the kids who were lost and what they meant to their parents and friends. The young man talked about how tragedy can change lives in an instant and how, for this reason, we need to live life every day.

After the assembly was over, my students and I somberly walked back to my classroom. You could have heard a pin drop in my room. No one was really looking at me – most likely because my emotions were showing on my face. After moments of silence, one of my students finally looked up at me and said that he could understand how hard it must have been for me to be at the assembly and hear that message. The silence was the only thing holding back the floodgates of my emotions; when it was broken, there was no way I could hide my feelings anymore. Several of my kids came up and gave me a hug. Inside, I was thinking of my two-year struggle to find direction after the sudden death of my teenage son, Blake. But on this day, I knew I was exactly where I was supposed to be.

The day I lost Blake seemed like any other normal day. It was a Friday, December 23rd, 2005. My wife and I owned two liquor stores and a laundromat in a small college town in western Kansas, and we renovated homes when time allowed. I had been divorced about five years from my first wife, leaving that relationship with only my son. On this Friday in late December, Blake was sweet sixteen and loving life and the social part of school. Like most teenagers, he didn't care much for the academic part (though he did his best).

At this time, my life and definition of family were changing in curious, but exciting ways. My current wife, Gena, and I had just been married in August of 2005. She brought into our marriage a very smart, focused, three-year-old boy named Jacob. Before meeting Gena, I had purchased an old, rundown home that was built in 1912, which at one time dominated a small area of town as one of the really large, gothic, Victorian homes. Allowing myself a little adventure as a single man, I purchased the house, daring to get in a little over my head. It was bank owned, had sat vacant for almost three years and had rapidly deteriorated. The house had no running water, no heat and was not livable. However, I like challenges and was up to the task of restoring this house to its previous luster.

Once Gena and I started dating, she and Blake hit it off right away. Blake loved Gena, her kindness and her thoughtful gestures. Gena took a sincere interest in Blake and his academic struggles; she thought so much of him. Gena's son, Jacob, looked up to Blake like a big brother, but both were young enough that I am not sure they really appreciated the depth of the relationship. In whatever he did, Blake was so loveable with his infectious smile and readiness to give a hug. Blake started bringing friends around to meet Gena. He would come in and puppy-dog up his big, blue eyes, bat his eyelashes a few times sincerely, and the next thing you know she was making them all something to eat. Blake and his friends felt very welcome at our house, and everybody was starting to enjoy these new family dynamics.

Life went on like that until that fateful Friday, December 23rd, 2005.

I knew our liquor stores would be busy that day and the next. I have always been an early riser, but I remember getting up even a little earlier than normal so I could be a step ahead for this particularly busy day. I was working at our smaller location that morning moving, stocking, and organizing things for the day, when Blake and a friend walked in the store. Oh, that smile. . . I can see it now. With his hands in his pockets, he had stopped in to say "hello" and ask if I needed any help. Appreciating this gesture, I kept him busy running errands for about an hour, and I think he wore that big, beautiful smile the whole time.

As he was finishing up, he told me he and his friend were going to do a little shopping before Christmas. I asked him if he had enough money before his answer (and that smile) solicited a little extra cash "just in case." As he started to leave, I asked him if he was sure he had enough. He just smiled again and said he thought he did. Of course, that response only gained him a little more money and off they went.

The day seemed to fly by. I was busy moving inventory and getting ready for one of the busiest Friday/Saturday combinations of the year due to the Christmas holiday being on Sunday and Kansas laws prohibiting sales of alcohol on Sundays. I had gone to our other store and was in the back room breaking down boxes when I turned around to see Blake standing in the doorway, still wearing that beautiful smile; I wish you could see it. He was standing with his arms spread open to give me a hug; he was having a wonderful day. He was out of school with his best friend, buying gifts and just being happy-go-lucky Blake.

I am pausing as I write this to take a few deep breaths; that moment in the liquor store was the last time I saw my sixteen-year-old son, Blake Christopher Munsch, alive.

I remember standing up to accept and return that same loving bear hug. Why was this hug so big and tight? He hugged me often, but this one was tighter and longer than most of the others. As I had him in my arms, squeezing him tightly, I asked him about school. His reply was that it was Christmas and we could talk about it after the holiday. I just smiled back at him, still nose-to-nose, and agreed. I told him that I loved him and he replied the same. He stepped back and I asked if he had had enough money for the gifts he meant to buy. His reply was that I had helped him so much already that he thought we were even.

"We were even" – that is not the typical answer from a sixteen-year-old boy who loved to have a little extra cash in his pocket. He always had things to buy, video games to rent or a soda to pick up for the ride. Those words still don't make complete sense to me. Did his spirit know what was happening? I have asked myself that question many times. I think it did, and he was quietly telling me goodbye.

I wish I'd have known that then.

He stepped out to finish up his shopping. He was headed to buy his mother a statue of a little boy kneeling at the feet of an angel with a plaque on the bottom that read, "I remember my father and mother's prayers and they have always followed me. They have clung to me all my life." I looked out the window and watched him walk to his car before I turned around and went back to work. I had no idea that in just a few short hours the world I had grown so accustomed to would be turned so completely upside down.

2. THE CALL

Men talk about sights, sounds or smells of war – how those thoughts will never leave them. They talk about these things like they happened yesterday, but it may have been forty years ago. I know how they feel; I can still hear the cry of a mother who has just been told her son was killed in a car wreck. I don't know if what happened was registering with me at that moment, but the sound of her anguish is something I will never forget; I wish I could.

It was around 10 P.M., and I was lying in bed somewhere between sleep and consciousness. The phone rang. I remember vividly picking it up and looking at caller-id to see who was calling. In my somewhat unconscious stare at the name I remember seeing it was a call from Blake's mother's house. I answered. A man's voice I did not recognize said, "Kris, Blake was in an accident tonight and did not make it." My thoughts were very confused because I was hearing a stranger's voice from his mother's house. Then I focused for a split second on the cry of my ex-wife in the background and it started to make sense. Before I could listen to another word, I handed the phone to Gena. I remember taking three steps from the bed and falling to my knees, doubled over, barely able to breathe. Gena listened on the phone for what seemed like an hour, but she says it was only long enough to hear the words herself. She went directly to the bathroom and began to vomit, but I don't remember that – we were worlds apart.

I was on my knees, doubled over looking for air. I took a couple of very deep breaths; I crawled back to the phone on the bed and dialed Blake's mom. The stranger's voice was now replaced by her husbands' voice, and again my attention focused on the cry of Blake's mother in the background. I needed to hear the words "Blake is gone" again; he confirmed it and I hung up the phone. After hearing this a second time, I lost all my strength and went straight back to my knees. I closed my eyes and asked God to take care of us, to please take Blake and protect him. To this day, I still am not sure why that was my first reaction. I remember thinking for a moment, *This is something I cannot do on my own; God is the only thing that might help me in a time like this.*

I stumbled around to find my clothes so I could go downstairs. There was a feeling of sickness consuming me that I will never forget. I knew I had to face this, but I didn't want to. The first people I called were our neighbors, Tom and Barb. They are good people, and had become extended family to me while I was renovating the house. When they answered, in a very shaky voice I asked if they could come over.

They appeared at the back door in an instant and I told them Blake had died in a car accident. I can still see the look on their faces. They have young children of their own, so they just stared at me in disbelief.   A moment later, Barb headed for Gena and Tom followed me into the kitchen so I could start making phone calls.

A MAN'S VOICE SAID, "KRIS, BLAKE WAS IN AN ACCIDENT TONIGHT AND DID NOT MAKE IT"

Strange what happens to the brain in these traumatic instances: some things are crystal clear and others are so vague they seem surreal, like they were scenes from some other person's life. Phone numbers that I knew by heart completely escaped me. As I looked through a drawer in the kitchen for a sheet that listed people's contact information, I remember Tom looking on, helplessly. It was as if I was so scattered no one could possibly help.

One of the first calls I made was to the police department requesting that the sheriff or trooper who had informed my ex-wife of the accident come by my house so I could speak to him. It seems strange, but I needed someone to walk through my door and tell me. When the officers arrived, I remember them parking in front of the house and walking up to the front door. I know they told me about the accident but I was numb, vacant, and my mind was going a thousand different directions. Here they stood telling a father his teenage son was gone forever; it just was not making sense.

According to police, Blake had been at home that evening and ventured out for a while with friends. He parked his car at a friend's house and somehow found himself in the driver's seat of another car with a friend in the passenger's seat. Blake's best friend was in the back seat along with two young ladies. They all ended up on an old road that leads east out of town. They drove right by the high school Blake attended and the street that lead just two blocks to his home before coming to a stop sign just east of town. He stopped at this one – why not the next? A few miles down the road, the blacktop ends and it turns into a gravel road. The intersecting north-south road is a paved one that comes off the interstate highway.

Blake drove right past that stop sign. At the moment he entered that intersection, an elderly lady was driving home, southbound, after celebrating an early Christmas with her family members. Had he waited just two more seconds at the previous stop sign, he would still be here today. I still tell myself the timing was meant to be because I don't know how else to look at it. The driver's door was positioned squarely in the center of the lane the lady was traveling. The car Blake was driving wrapped around the front of the woman's vehicle, killing him instantly; his death certificate says he died within seconds, and I hope that's true. The impact was horrific; both vehicles were driven by the force into the east ditch. The lady's car spun around and ended up backwards in the ditch, breaking both her feet and pinning her in the car.

The other kids in the car with Blake were all injured. After the car was hit, it flew into the ditch and struck a stone post, which made the car flip over. Blake's best friend directly behind him just missed the total impact by inches; he was left unconscious and in critical condition. The other kids also suffered broken bones and were in serious condition. A few days after the accident, I asked a fireman who was at the scene to tell me what he saw. I didn't want to know, but I needed to know. He said that Blake died instantly. When I asked him how he knew, he said with a hesitant voice that when he crawled into the car to remove Blake, his eyes were wide open, which signified that it happened quickly. It was really hard to hear these details, but I wanted to know everything so I could move forward in some kind of meaningful way.

3. THE HARDEST STEP

I woke early on Saturday morning after the previous day's level of mental exhaustion and emotional stress forced me to succumb to sleep. The sun was coming up, and people were just waking to their Christmas Eve obligations and last-minute shopping; the world was giving no indication that it was anything other than "business as usual." But my son was dead, and I didn't really know what I was supposed to be doing. I was looking for a familiar routine and was having trouble finding it. Little did I know there would be nothing routine about my life ever again.

I abandoned routine and decided I needed to see where the accident had happened. I called Danny, a close friend of mine, and asked if he would go with me. To this day, I don't know what I was looking for – I guess I just needed to be there and see it for myself, but I was scared to death inside. For whatever reason, I would soon find myself standing in that intersection.

As we approached the location of the accident, fear ran rampant inside of me and I was torn between wanting to look, but not wanting to see. The marks on the road were visible, and fence posts were scattered about in the ditch and beyond. Here I was, in the early hours of dawn, standing in the intersection where my son had given up his life just a few short hours before. This was the place he took his last breath. This was the place his spirit left this earth. I didn't want to be anywhere else and at the exact same time, I wanted to be as far from here as possible. I have never felt this level of fear or confusion before, or since, in my life. It was time to leave.

This was not how I had pictured my Christmas Eve. That evening we were supposed to have our Christmas as a family, but in a sudden twist of metal and fate, I would instead spend that morning viewing my son's corpse and discussing funeral details. That morning after I got home from the site of the accident, Gena and I sat on the couch just looking at each other in silence. Gena was terrified of what would happen next – I don't know how else to explain it. Things would never be the same again. We were both in the same situation, feeling that same pressure, tension and loss. What do you say? How do you act?

At 9 A.M., we left to meet the funeral director. Gena and I drove with our neighbor, Tom, to the funeral home. Tom wanted to come along for support; I have never asked him how hard that was. The silence in the truck on the ride to the funeral home did little to make this more real in my mind; this was still a dream to me and was not a part of any reality my mind could fathom. As we pulled in front of the funeral home, I felt very cold and scared. I had driven by this place a million times without even glancing at it, and I certainly never imagined standing here under these circumstances. I was about to see my son of sixteen years, the boy I had cared for, played catch with, and taken to movies, but I was about to see him deceased. How does a parent's brain process the thought of seeing his child's body, knowing the life and light that were inside have been extinguished?

As we entered the funeral home, the director met us and was a true gentleman. I was shaking hands with a man who had worked all night to make my son presentable to me. He told me, almost apologetically, that Blake's injuries were bad. That should have been hard to hear, but at that point I was hardly processing words.

He pointed to a door and indicated that Blake was in that room. I think I heard him say whenever I was ready we could go in. I would never be ready. I didn't want to be ready, and I wanted time to stop. I wanted this all to just stop. I turned and walked toward the door, but I am still not sure what was making my legs move.

I stopped at the door, taking inventory of my numbness. My legs did not want to take another step because my life would change with the next step. I had taken millions of steps before, but I was about to take one step that would change everything. I had already been told the news in a phone call. I had stood in my home and listened to the officers tell me the news. I had gone to the accident scene and witnessed the marks on the road and the evidence in the ditch. But this next step would make it more final than anything else.

I stood just outside the doorway knowing that the next step would make all I had been told the previous twelve hours an undeniable part of my story – a part of who I would become. Just beyond that threshold was a reality that would change everything I had come to know and believe into a life I did not recognize. I was horrified. Gena and Tom stood behind me waiting patiently, and since there was no other option, I took that next step.

Words cannot explain the wash of emotion that filled my body. This experience poured through my veins. I don't know if it was truly emotion or if it was part of my spirit, part of who I am, but the feeling that overtook me was a physical sensation. It brushed my skin and flowed across my chest. It went up from my feet, through my body, and left my head, and it felt like someone was holding a fan pointed directly at me. This may sound strange, but now I know what I felt was my previous life leaving, and nobody is prepared for the emptiness that follows.

I walked up to Blake and felt his hair. I put my hand on the dark blue, velvet blanket that covered him and felt what I hoped I would not. Blake was gone forever and nothing would bring him back. I just kept thinking that I was doing things a father should never have to do and that this is not how life is supposed to be. I was experiencing so many thoughts and emotions, but I was trying hard to be in control; I was used to being in control.

And it is only now, as I look back, I see that losing control is a necessary growing pain. Only now do I realize that the hardest step is the one we have to take when there are just no other options left.

4. SCATTERED

I had spent a lifetime building who I was, and losing Blake had never been part of the life I had planned. The thought of losing a child may cross your mind, but parents try desperately to dismiss and avoid these fears. The fear itself seems too painful, but this was real; he was gone, and losing control had never been part of who I was. Now I had to accept that the person I had spent all those years working to become was no more. In times of crisis, people change. Whether the change is deliberate or the effect of circumstances, some kind of growth is inevitable in life. In my case, change came without asking. Until the moment I walked though the door at the funeral home, I was in control of my identity, my family, my businesses and my life.

Now every piece of me I had spent a lifetime accumulating was scattered to the winds. Now, on this Christmas Eve morning, I was standing in a funeral home looking at my son who had been killed in a violent car accident not even twelve hours ago. That did not process well – crisis usually doesn't. I vividly remember this feeling that came right stepping through the door and losing my breath upon seeing Blake's body – that feeling was *get in control of this*.

My mind was racing between the details and events of the last twelve hours, which made no sense, and longing for the details and routines of my old life, which made perfect sense. I'm ashamed to admit that my thoughts jumped between what had happened to Blake and all the emotional heaviness that came with that, to the day-to-day business concerns of what I was supposed to be doing on this busy day to prepare the stores for last-minute shoppers. I'm ashamed, but I also know this is common – we long for control and normality in times of chaos and confusion. That's how we survive.

My mind was immediately full of so many unanswerable questions: *Who was involved? Where is the car? Where are the other kids? Who was the person in the other car and how badly was she injured? Is my family coming to town? Are the other families ok?* All these questions were bouncing around my head simultaneously and I was trying very hard to process everything. Who was going to answer these questions, and when? I just couldn't tame my wild thoughts or know what I was supposed to do next, so I did what came natural to me. I tried my best to keep up.

Keeping my mind busy with details meant I could put off accepting the fate of my son as long as possible. I think it was a natural defense mechanism. What is strange looking back is that I distinctly remember trying to comfort everyone else. I even went so far as to contact the patrolman who had worked the accident to let him know that I was available if he needed someone to talk to. I have no idea if this is common or not, but the person I thought I was – that "in control" person – thought it was my job to let everyone know I was fine and would survive this. I had spent a lifetime being in control, so why would I stop now?

For my own sake, when was I going to stop denying what was happening to me? Not anytime soon: I was still ready to prove everyone wrong. It was like I thought, *If I only glance at the issue, is it happening?* If a tree falls in the woods, it makes a sound, whether we are there to hear it or not, and the view of my forest had been drastically changed, whether I wanted to acknowledge it or not. Blake was now lying in a grave, not at home in his bed, and no amount of denial or attention to daily details was going to undo that truth. Nevertheless, I continued to ignore how scattered I felt and tried to remain in control. To me, everything I was doing was the only way to do it.

In my search for control, I was still secretly hoping to prove everyone wrong, and in my mind, I needed more proof. I called the county sheriff and asked if I could see the car. He told me that he would take me to see the car but asked if it was necessary. He was very nice and told me that I should think about it for a couple of days and get back with him if I still wanted to see it. The car was bad, and he wondered what I would gain by seeing it. The more he was taking control from me, the more I wanted control and was determined to see the car.

It was almost exactly forty-eight hours since I had asked to see the car when I called the sheriff again and left word to call me. He called, and this time instead of telling him I wanted to see the car, I told him I *needed* to see the car. A sheriff's deputy I had known for quite some time (and, sadly, with whom Blake had done a "ride along" just a few months earlier while exploring the possibility of becoming a police officer) picked me up at my house and took me to a plain, metal building with no markings on it. We pulled in and talked for a few minutes outside the building, but the scattered thoughts continued to race around in my head, and I'm pretty sure I was close to short-circuiting.

In the back corner of the building sat the car, and for a moment, the scattered thoughts stopped. It was absolute destruction. Not a piece of metal on the car was in its intended shape. As much as I wanted to look away, I couldn't; this is why I was here. I wanted to remain in control and finally accept whether or not this horrible chapter of my life was really happening, and the evidence was right in front of me.

My thoughts no longer raced, and if they had been, I just wouldn't have cared about keeping up with them anymore. My whole being felt physically sick, instantly and violently. I knew that my previous life had permanently left – and with it left all semblance of control over the life I had once known.

5. REALIZATION

Somehow, life continued as best it (and I) could.

As I drove home from the store one afternoon a couple of weeks after the loss of Blake, something happened. I started to feel tightness in my chest, and my vision started to close. I got home as quickly as I could. Stumbling into the house, I told Gena to get me a bag of some sort as I headed for the couch. I sat with my head back and slowly breathed into the bag. I'm not sure what triggered it, but I needed to breathe deeply to calm myself down. I don't know if it was fatigue or stress, but something was telling me I was going through a major transformation.

And I was fighting it every step of the way.

After Blake's death, I knew my world had changed, but I didn't understand why I needed to change. I thought I could still be the same person because these things are happening *around* me, not *to* me. Even though I knew things had changed in my life, I was bound and determined that everything was going to stay the same. Or was it? Everywhere I drove and everywhere I went, things were different.

And as silly as it sounds, it was like everything, from the largest to the smallest detail, was changing all around me. I remember thinking, as I showered the morning of Blake's funeral, that showering would never be the same. Here was a dad taking a shower so that he could go to his son's funeral. I remember reaching into the drawer to pull out my toothbrush and toothpaste, and realizing that even this would be different for the rest of my life. I stood in front of the mirror looking at the tube of toothpaste and thought, *This tube will run out and I will need a new one, but I can't get a new tube of toothpaste; this is the tube I had when Blake was still alive.* Everything was now suddenly categorized into two bins – life before Blake's death and life after. I was trying so desperately to cling to all the items in that first bin that I was ignoring that the second one was here – and noticeably empty.

I distinctly remember my family picking up the phrase "new normal" in our lives. I have no idea where this phrase came from, but wherever I picked it up, it was so true. If I am looking for a new normal, how exactly does the old normal fit? How many new things must I do to become a new me?

That was my life then: more questions than answers. I was (and still am) full of questions about this new normal. After crisis, you have to learn to adjust to the new life you are living, and I did not go gentle into that new life. I still wanted to be in control of my destiny – still wanted to be in control of my mourning – I wanted to rage against the dying of my old life.

> I STILL WANTED TO BE IN CONTROL OF MY DESTINY - STILL WANTED TO BE IN CONTROL OF MY MOURNING - I WANTED TO RAGE AGAINST THE DYING OF MY OLD LIFE

I sit here writing today and actually chuckle to think that I was ever going to do these steps my way. How foolish a man was I. These steps happen in good time and when you least expect them to happen because you are just way too scattered (call it what you will) to move through them on your own. What started to occur while I was going through all this was the realization that in order to fit in this new life where I had been placed, I needed to start working on a new me.

Suddenly, it was like I could see both of those imaginary bins and take a serious look at who I was before I lost Blake as well as who I needed to be to make sense of my life without him. I was scrambling to bring some sort of normal to the life I shared with my quickly changing family. I had been married only four months before, and I had a stepson who was living with this new, altered me in his life.

In my mind, the best way to redefine myself and reestablish some control was to sell everything and move to a new town with a new house and a new job. I thought if everything around me was new, it would be easier to feel that this really was a new normal – a new life.

I have never read what experts recommend after you lose someone or go through a life crisis. I remember hearing from several people that one should not make any changes for six months, two years, three years, etc. I see the logic in that statement, but what these "experts" don't realize is the changes have already happened. You *are* the new person in the house or the new guy in town because the change after a crisis has already taken place inside your own reality – external factors within your control have no bearing on this real sense that things are different.

I was sure that if I could change external features to match my internal reality I could reinvent myself. I could feel in my heart that I wanted to be something different. After years of taking old houses and bringing them back to life, how difficult could this life-renovation be? I would soon find out moving a wall and picking paint swatches is not exactly the same thing as rebuilding a life. In the past I could always find materials to make my vision become a reality, but in all the lumberyards and building supply stores I've frequented, I've never found a "new life" section. I was on my own.

I continued to live like the old me, pretending to be the new me. We decided to move to another city and purchase a business; surely, that change would make everything better. My wife and I would operate our new business together, and I was convinced the old me would fit in this new environment, even if I was doing things the same old way. I tried this pattern several times in several places before I figured out that it wasn't working; this was still external change, and I needed to accept my internal change.

> I COULD FEEL IN
> MY HEART THAT
> I WANTED TO
> BE SOMETHING
> DIFFERENT

Finally, I did. I woke up one night and this sick, empty feeling in my stomach told me that the path I was on sounded good, but it wasn't fitting. I felt exactly like a two-year-old child sitting in front of the little toy that you fit the multi-shaped pegs into the corresponding holes, except that I was feeling that perplexed in this adult body. There I sat, trying so hard to fit this old, square peg into a round and continuously shrinking reality. Even if I could have made it fit, would it have looked and felt right? Of course not. Looking back now, I can tell you that it may go in if you force it, but that is not how it was intended. You have to find the right peg for the right hole, and, after crisis, this is very difficult.

This is when it all started to sink in. After deciding to walk away from being a business owner again, I needed to do something drastic. Losing control of my destiny, my life, and my family was extremely difficult, but this needed to happen. The obligations I was in charge of before didn't seem important to me anymore. I wanted Gena to tell me what to do. This inner turmoil continued to boil – and threatened to boil over into my relationships as I looked for answers. *Why can't someone tell me what to do? Will someone please give me a road map of who I am supposed to be?*

> OUR FAMILY CIRCLE HAD JUST TIGHTENED AND THERE I STOOD, TELLING HER I WANTED TO KILL MYSELF

Some people may know the depths one can feel when they lose their identity and their sense of control, but I reached new lows. I was leaving the house one day and I was franticly hoping for something to make sense. Gena asked me something along the lines of where my head was – I don't remember exactly. My response to her was that if I had the ability or courage, I would kill myself. She just stood there looking at me in disbelief. She had just become a part of my new life and helped me through Blake's death; our family circle had just tightened and there I stood, telling her I wanted to kill myself.

To this day, I remember that moment and her reaction so vividly that I am unimaginably sorry that I could have said such a hurtful, frightening thing to someone I love. I had just reached a point where I could not imagine living the rest of my life in such turmoil, so at that moment, ending it all seemed like a move in a positive direction.

This is how hard it can be to let go of a life that you once knew to move toward what (and whom) you might eventually become in the life that is all around you. It's a simple survival lesson, but in order to reach a new destination, a castaway must leave the comfort of the island and hope for the best. If not, eventually the tide will take him against his will.

6. TRANSITIONS

Transition happens all the time in the cycle of life and companies. Going through a transition in the workplace may not be easy, but company strategies guide this kind of change. Usually, change is introduced by someone with a vision before co-workers and associates adopt these practices. Eventually, everyone encourages one another to work toward the vision and change begins to occur collectively. As a piece in this puzzle, much of your time is spent following the examples of others and making your own personal contributions to the shared vision.

Going through a personal tragedy does not typically allow for this group effect to happen, so transition can be lonely. You are experiencing change personally and the tragedy affects everyone differently. This loss affected my wife dearly because Blake and Gena had grown very close. However, it was also different because he was not her flesh and blood.

I lost my son. I lost a boy I watched grow up. I lost someone I spent a lifetime worrying about. I worried about his grades. I worried about the friends he had. I worried about everything parents worry about. I worried about leaving him with the lessons and security he would need to survive if I were taken from this earth. In the end, all this worrying didn't save Blake. It makes sense: the things you prepare for are never the ones that get you, and life is full of surprises.

I had prepared for a lifetime of worry, vigilance, protection, guidance, nurturing, learning, and (at the right times and in the right doses) leadership. Then, all of a sudden, that part of my identity was no longer intact, and that part of my life no longer made sense. Those worries were over. It's probably very similar to what one feels after living in the same home for sixteen years before it is suddenly destroyed in a tornado. Everything I had grown to know was now scattered across a field of memories, and the pieces would never be the same again.

During this time of insanity and searching, I spent many hours in the basement of our home looking on the Internet for all sorts of jobs. I would look endlessly at all sorts of positions, thinking *There has to be something out there that can fix me.* One late evening as I sat staring at the computer, Gena came down the stairs and sat looking at me. She had something to say, and I didn't know if I wanted to hear it. She told me that she and Jacob had been upstairs patiently waiting for me to become a part of their lives again. She told me that I needed to start figuring out what I was going to do because there were still two people who were very much alive, and they needed me.

At first I became very defensive; in my opinion, I had been doing all I could. In my head I had done many things, but I was still far from being in control. Her words were a turning point for me; the words "we need you back in our lives" shook me because in my mind I didn't even realize I had left. Reality set in, and I now knew that the doorbell was not going to ring just so somebody on the other side could tell me how to get my life back. I had to get up and create that plan myself. I had to get off that island and swim back to civilization and the people who needed me, regardless of how strong the current was.

I needed to get back into the world and be around people again. I applied for a desk job and was hired. Looking back, the slightest flicker of success was like a beacon. During the day I worked in a very quiet cubical, doing my best to make positive progress. Along with the job, I took some classes at the local university. I discovered that I loved going to school and the process of learning something new, and for the first time in a long time it felt like something fit without having to force it. School was breathing fresh life into me.

This new life gave those around me hope that I was starting to see a brighter future. As difficult as it felt on my side of the fence, I cannot imagine the view others had of what I was going through. I am sure they found my professional misadventures curious, and perhaps many more thought they knew exactly what I needed to be doing. Like most people with addictions, I was trying to get one last fix of that old life I had when I was Blake's father and a successful business owner. And like most people with addictions, I needed to be honest with myself before I could change. Forgive the expression, but denial is a bitch.

I'll be forever grateful that my wife not only patiently allowed me to discover myself, but that she also let me know that my success mattered to more people than just myself.

There is a big difference between finding yourself and getting to know yourself. It took me a while to see that knowing myself internally was the only way any external reality was going to make sense – it never works the other way around.

Shortly after Gena had spoken these words to me, I received a phone call from my family telling me the date for what would have been Blake's high school graduation and the news that the school planned to honor Blake by leaving his place in the seating arrangement open in his memory. Fortunately, I was starting to know the limits of how much reminiscing I could (or was willing to) handle.

I chose not to attend, but was told that his graduation would be broadcast online. I wanted to look, but at the same time I didn't want to, and I felt torn. Finally, I decided to err on the side of looking and deal with the consequences later. I turned on the computer and as the camera scanned the floor, I saw it. There was Blake's chair, with cap and gown draped over the seat. On the seat lay a rose. It was a gesture of love and respect from his classmates, symbolizing that they missed him.

For a split second, it felt like my heart stopped.

Like all things that happen are meant to be, watching this was meant to be, but I'm so glad I wasn't there in person. I cried and then I cried some more. I looked again, and I cried again. Blake's graduation was the final evidence that I was walking this walk still holding on to the past; my son was truly gone. It was time to completely accept this transition from past to present, and my family couldn't continue to be stuck in the middle of then and now.

On the night Blake died, I told Gena, "All along I was trying to teach Blake lessons about life, but it was he who was going to teach me the most." When I said those words that night I thought I knew what they meant. It wasn't until I started to accept my new normal that I realized how much this truth would impact me, and how it would help me find my way out of the darkness and off the island.

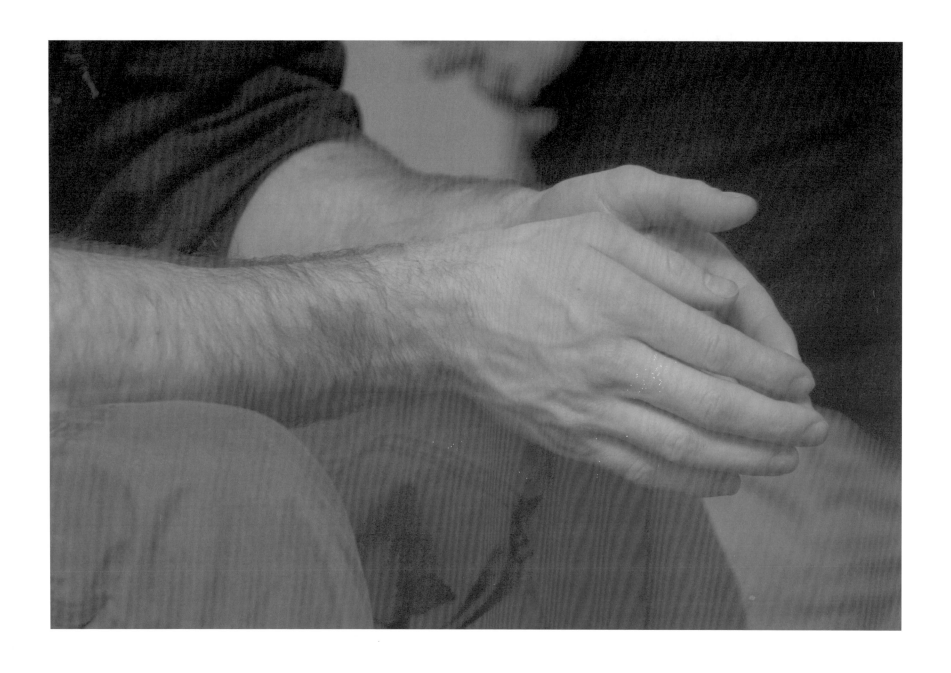

7. ACCEPTING CRISIS

Until I started writing this book, I thought my crisis was losing my son. Looking back now, losing Blake was my tragedy, but my crisis was my inability to adapt to my new life without him. Losing a young man with so much to offer seemed like an impossible blow to overcome, but this was just a temporary circumstance. The crisis was the loss of identity and direction I felt, neither of which is unique to my circumstances. Similar loss and crisis can be felt in divorce, death, or any other personal tragedy beyond our control.

My crisis began right after the funeral ended and my house emptied. It was obvious I was in crisis because I was willing to sell off the businesses we had worked so hard to build and leave behind a life that afforded us many things we don't have today. Possessions that previously mattered quickly became unimportant during my crisis. My mini-crisis actually began before I had lost Blake, although it took me a while to figure this out. My crisis might have actually started with my divorce.

As much as divorce can save two people from a life of unhappiness, mine felt tragic. For the first few years after the divorce, I struggled to find an identity outside of that relationship. Suddenly, things that defined me before my divorce were no longer a part of my life, and a new identity was slowly emerging through my work in town and the name I was making for myself. I was becoming a local businessman with good ideas that worked, and over time I earned my bankers' unwavering faith in my ability to see a project through. My new life seemed to be coming together.

After Blake's death, my sudden willingness to quickly abandon that identity I had spent so much time building helped me understand that changing external realities is never a long-term fix for the struggles going on inside my head, and once again (but this time with Gena and Jacob in tow) I had to ask myself, *Who am I?*

One of the most productive steps I made after Blake's death was making this distinction between the circumstance of Blake's death (which was tragic and beyond my control) and the identity crisis I felt after this loss (which was a humbling and painful growth spurt in disguise). I wasted a lot of time wondering when my identity was going to magically rise from the ashes of this tragedy like a Phoenix and reveal my purpose in the world. Once I accepted that I was dealing with my personal loss of identity, I stopped asking questions and looking for answers on the outside. Soul searching, after all, can only be done in one place.

As I watched Blake's graduation online, his vacant chair adorned with cap and gown and rose, the familiar old question was still with me – *Who am I?* Almost in response to my silent question, the teacher Blake's senior class had invited to give the graduation address stepped forward to talk about what teaching had meant to her. She talked about how she felt she had made a difference to dozens of kids over the years and how rewarding it felt to give something back to society and her community. Her passion for teaching and learning was instantly contagious, and when her speech concluded, I felt she had been speaking to me.

I could not get her words out of my thoughts for the rest of the evening. Gena and Jacob were gone, so I took this opportunity to sit in silence and think about what I had just heard. In that stillness, the first interruption in a long patch of chaos, I had time to sit and reflect about what had happened the past year and a half, as well as time to reflect on the identity crisis Blake's tragic death had caused.

The following day would have been Blake's eighteenth birthday, so the stillness in my mind was short-lived. Turning eighteen should be a special time to celebrate children becoming adults, but our day was far from joyous. I attempted to go to work, only to find myself quietly shedding tears throughout the day. I needed to return to my ground zero. Standing at Blake's graveside on his eighteenth birthday, trying to answer a million questions about who I am and what I'm supposed to be doing, I felt something I hadn't felt in a long time. Out of nowhere, this no one was given the gift of direction.

Just three years before, in an identity search after my divorce, I completed my teaching degree. My degree was in the area of woodworking and drafting. I needed to teach. I needed to be around kids. I needed that challenge because I felt passionate about making a difference. It was like a light had turned on, and I could not drive fast enough to the university to talk to one of my professors. I had nothing to lose and only life to gain. It wasn't like I wanted this identity to fit – it was like I couldn't think of anything else worth trying. From my soul, the feelings I had over not being able to help my son were finally giving me some direction, and my body finally got the message – this was me.

First I had surrounding doubt to deal with, and I had earned every bit of it. After spending almost two years being indecisive in my struggle to find new direction for my life and family, Gena was less than enthusiastic about this new venture. Even my trusted professor looked at me with a sideways glance when I told him my plan. I felt teaching was something beyond what I wanted to do; I *needed* to teach. I had lost my son, but this would give me the opportunity to feel that responsibility again and potentially help hundreds in return. I had found something I was passionate about, and I was ready to leave this crisis behind and embrace this identity.

I had let those around me down so often they had grown pretty uncertain of my decision-making ability, but I knew what I was feeling, and this felt right. My own internal confusion subsided and the questions that had been echoing inside my head were suddenly silenced. The confusion and the loss I felt started to fade. The craziness of having no idea who I was anymore gave way to more stability and certainty with each and every day I thought about being in the classroom around kids.

I had found a new, meaningful way to fill the void left by Blake's absence, and I was ready to become a mentor to countless kids. But I had taken the most necessary (and also the most difficult) step when I stopped running long enough to look in the mirror. Part of getting to know myself was seeing every side of me, and in order to move forward, I needed to spend a little time sorting through the dusty corners of the past to ensure that the mistakes I'd made wouldn't be repeated.

I had to open myself up and be honest about my regrets.

8. REGRETS

Living without regret is just not possible. People may say that they live life with no regrets, but in my opinion, that is just not feasible unless you are perfect or have no conscience. Everyone wishes they could have a "do-over" at least once; that's regret.

After Blake died, I felt I'd never get the opportunity to make up for the regrets I had, and that made it really tough to forgive myself for those shortcomings. Over time, I've learned the importance of separating these two emotions. I can't get a "do-over" with my son, but I can work on forgiving myself. While the regrets can never be erased, they become less painful once you choose to learn from those missteps and commit to living your life with as few as possible from that moment forward. And the great thing is, whether you are trying to cope with crisis or not, it is never too late to start.

I remember so clearly something that happened right after losing Blake. As I came down the wooden staircase that overlooked the entryway, I saw my three-year-old stepson, Jacob, playing with his toy trains underneath a large picture window. He loved those trains, but would often become frustrated hooking them together. When Jacob saw me on the stairs, he asked for help hooking the two little trains together. What crossed my mind was the real thought that helping him hook those trains together is something I wished I would have done so much more of when Blake was little, and since guilt is such an evil monster, I actually asked myself if hooking Jacob's trains together would be cheating Blake in some way. I quickly answered my own question by kneeling down beside Jacob and not only hooking them together, but also by taking the time to teach him so he could do it.

I know how crazy that first thought sounds, but I'm not ashamed to admit it. These thoughts are a normal part of the struggle to make sense of circumstances that just don't seem to

> **REGRETS BECOME LESS PAINFUL WHEN WE LEARN FROM THEM AND COMMIT TO LIVE LIFE WITH AS FEW AS POSSIBLE FROM THAT MOMENT FORWARD**

make sense. Now I am grateful that I had those thoughts because they gave me a much-needed jumpstart into facing my regrets. And I needed that because dealing with regret is very uncomfortable.

Shortly after Blake's death, I was asked by my family if I had regrets, and I told them no. I felt I had done all I could for him. That answer was just my way of remaining in control of my emotions and thoughts: of denying anything to do with my failures as Blake's dad. But by admitting these regrets, I was able to say "never again," and use that small affirmation to make each day a little better than the last.

It is so simple; if you have regret, face it. Tell the people affected that you are sorry and use that sorrow to move forward, resolving never to offend that same way again. Turn your sorrow into good deeds and make a difference in the rest of your life. Nothing can be as regrettable as knowing how to do things the right way and still doing them the wrong way. It is easier said than done because we are human, but through humility comes growth.

I learned a lot about myself by accepting my faults and working to live by these small, emerging affirmations of the person I was starting to become. I felt that, slowly, I was getting to know the new me and was starting to understand what kind of work I was supposed to be doing.

PEOPLE WHO HAVE EXPERIENCED
TRAGEDY HAVE THE ABILITY TO
DO AND SAY GREAT THINGS

9. AFFIRMATION AND GOALS

Grieving people need a reason to snap out of their crisis and assert control over their own lives. Gena telling me that she and Jacob needed me was just the wake-up call I was waiting for, but I also think people have the power to give themselves wake-up calls.

It's a bit like being on a diet (and I'm speaking from experience here). A few years ago, I was depressed and spending many days in my basement staring at a computer screen waiting for someone else to come and save me. Besides having a keyboard in front of me, I also had food. It was my best feel-good solution for the moment, and it worked. No one was telling me to stop, so I continued to eat. Through this depression and experience, I found so much comfort in eating that it was taking a toll on my body. I needed to lose twenty-five pounds and I knew I needed to get it done, but the motivation was not there. I had no personal commitment to losing the weight, so it was not going to happen.

I think the same thing happens when we go through a tragedy and find ourselves in crisis. Unless we have found something that will give us direction and a reason to move forward, we will continue to fall back into routines and habits of the past. For this reason, I found that small affirmations really helped me address the regrets I had about the type of father I had been to Blake.

An affirmation is a statement we make that affirms who we are or what we intend to do. It is a way of holding ourselves accountable by stating our code of conduct and following personal principles when honoring our commitments. It took me a while to find an affirmation for my new life, but most of my delay stemmed from an unwillingness to take an honest look at who I was and what I was feeling. Until I could clearly see what direction my life was headed and what type of crisis I was dealing with, how could I move forward? People don't like to hear it, but we have to face our regrets in order to find a way to the new person we want to become.

In my own circumstances, Gena was my wake-up call, but I had to be willing to be accountable. Imagine you're a bus driver and everyone getting on the bus thinks they are headed to Las Vegas. They all get on and when they wake up, they notice they are in Mexico. After you do this a few times, passengers are going to get a little nervous when they get on because they have bought a ticket from you before. I knew this was how my wife felt, and I wasn't willing to let her down anymore. But I also had to realize that she wasn't really anxious to believe in me again – she'd ridden that bus for two years. Accountability had to come from me; I had to know what affirmations I had made, and I had to trust that, over time, following these principles would earn her trust again.

My affirmation took me almost three years to state. I not only needed to get the confidence of my family back that the things I was doing were being pursued with long-term commitment, but I needed to convince myself. It is natural to lose confidence after tragedy and crisis. The amount of work your mind is doing in order to adjust makes it impossible to make too many new commitments, let alone keep the old ones.

In order to jumpstart this new life, I adopted the affirmation that because I survived my tragedy, I have the power to do and say great things. After I told him about my struggle to find purpose following Blake's death, one of my professors shared these words with me. I did not feel like I had the power to do anything for the longest time. Instead, I felt as if tragedy had scarred me for life and I would always be the dad who lost his son. It took me a while to figure it out, but one of the worst things a person can do is mistake their tragedy for their identity.

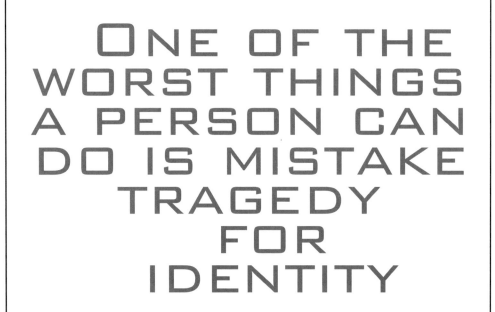

ONE OF THE WORST THINGS A PERSON CAN DO IS MISTAKE TRAGEDY FOR IDENTITY

I am the father who lost his son, but that in no way has taken away my abilities. As time has continued and I have learned not only who I am, but also what I want out of life, I've also learned that the abilities I have can be used in effective and powerful ways. This is only possible because I am aware of what I want and I am willing to learn from my regrets. From my crisis, I was able to get to know myself and leave the old ideas of who I was behind; this dismissal enabled me to become a new person in these new circumstances. Every crisis has this same transformative power.

The experience you go through in crisis is actually just life training you will never get anywhere else. I miss my son so much, but I feel blessed to have survived this chapter of my life, and I feel that way only because I experienced remarkable growth by coming out of this tragedy. Now I have the ability to reflect on the best and worst aspects of who I am and make appropriate adjustments to improve myself and the relationships I build with the people around me.

Because I have made the affirmation that my experience enables me to do and say great things, I set goals to hold myself accountable. This has been with me ever since I determined I wanted to be a better person for those people who are still in my life. Setting goals helps me know my feet are firmly on the path and helps my loved ones see that this is long-term and real this time. The more goals I can set and accomplish, the more trust I regain.

I want to take a minute to talk about goals here because I think more needs to be said about the value of giving your life a plan. Working with young kids every day, I know that they have a lot of dreams, but they have a hard time breaking those big dreams down into little, manageable goals. Goals are simply a measuring stick for how much progress you are making toward the life you envision for yourself. I heard a great quote about this once, so I'll paraphrase it: goals are a way of telling you how to spend your time rather than wondering where all of your time went. If I could give everyone I meet the instant faith in setting goals and striving for what they want one small step at a time, I think I would know a lot of people who felt they were living more fulfilling lives.

When I received my first teaching assignment, my first goal was to provide an exciting learning environment filled with opportunity. Given my circumstances, you would think that being a constant rock to my family would have been my first goal, but it was not. I was still a pebble rolling in a fast-moving stream, and I knew that every goal accomplished would have the added benefit of showing my family I was becoming a rock. I accomplished the goal of getting my shop in order (which was exciting to me), and thought that my own excitement about this new place might excite the kids.

My next goal was to survive the first semester (a common goal among new teachers, I assure you). People who knew me before the tragedy most likely had office pools going as to how long I would last, but they didn't understand how I'd grown. Many things I was doing in my new life were related to my old life, but the focus had changed. I knew my passion and worked on my weaknesses. I no longer mistook my tragedy for my identity. I was letting the internal me find a fitting external reality instead of hoping it would work the other way. I was also pursuing single goals instead of multiple goals at one time. These minor adjustments to my perspective and priorities made this major transition from the old me to the new me start to become reality.

> # GOALS ARE A WAY OF TELLING YOU HOW TO SPEND YOUR TIME RATHER THAN WONDERING WHERE ALL OF YOUR TIME WENT

Each goal I reached started to build my confidence as a teacher, but also as a husband and stepfather. My relationship with my stepson started to grow and we became much closer because I was allowing myself to reach out again. I was not as afraid to get rejected because I was becoming more aware of who I was. Kids can sense when things are not right, and after the accident, Jacob was just as reserved as I was. As I opened up, so did he.

Even now, my goals continue to build on the previous ones. Small goals have turned into larger goals and I try to manage two or three at a time. Instead of goals just focused on me and my survival, I can now look outside myself and help accomplish the goals of those around me.

Remember: no matter what it is, successfully rebuilding something always comes back to being honest about your strengths and weaknesses before you begin.

Today, instead of a pebble rolling out of control in a fast-moving stream, I sense the water moving around me. I am starting to grow into that rock and am feeling myself settling in my place. I have never been so passionate about life and what it has to offer as I am today. Of course, I still miss Blake horribly. But can you imagine the hurt in my heart if I was not doing something positive with this loss?

I can do and say great things because that is what Blake would want me to do with my life. Living by these words, I can change lives for the better. It may only be one life at a time, but over time these changes will multiply. If I hadn't decided to live by this affirmation, my life would be unbearable, and probably still in some form of crisis. Knowing these things is what keeps this rock in its place, and this knowledge is all the motivation I need to reach my goals today, tomorrow, and as long as this life allows me.

10. Shelter

As I have moved through this identity crisis in my life, I look back at what has been a solid reminder to me that this fight is worthwhile. What is it that has made me feel comfortable enough to lie down at night and sleep?

One of Blake's favorite movies was *Cast Away*, so it is ironic I sit here today writing about survival. I'll never know if that was another way his spirit was trying to tell me something; if so, I think I needed to be at this point in my life to realize what the movie was saying.

We are all familiar with the plot of *Cast Away*. This man is just zipping through the air with no intention of anything but reaching his destination. Obviously, he doesn't; his cargo plane crashes in a new world and he is expected to survive with what he has on board. This is very much like what you experience when tragedy strikes and find yourself in the emotional storm of crisis. Before you do anything else, you need to find shelter.

In the movie he finds a cave, and through horrible storms and difficult days, he uses this for shelter. It was all he had at the time and it was all he needed. In crisis, the things we once thought were critical to survival are no longer as important as we thought, and we start to look at the basic presences in our life which protect us.

In the movie, Tom Hanks' character befriends a volleyball he names (appropriately enough) Wilson. He felt that his obligation to this "other" would help him survive. In fact, during the climactic scene where he finally dares to leave the island on a raft, Wilson goes overboard, and Hanks' character risks his own life to bring Wilson (the volleyball) back to the safety of the raft.

While it may seem humorous or far-fetched, it is also instructive. His obligation to Wilson kept him alive for several years. In order to push through his crisis, he needed to be accountable to someone other than himself, and this accountability was one of the keys to his survival. He also chose to save one package, adorned with a butterfly, he found washed up on the beach after the crash. He made a commitment to himself to deliver that package. All the other packages became resources that were utilized to survive. This is similar to the experience I went through when my obligations changed without my understanding why. Attaching yourself to a single goal can lead you from crisis.

I have been in that crisis. I wasn't literally on an island, but I've been out there, seemingly by myself, searching for a way back to civilization and a life that makes sense. As my battle for survival has continued, my family has become my "Wilson" (they'd laugh at this comparison), and when I think about all that sustained me during this struggle, I also know that my wife's love, patience and support acted as my shelter. These are what made me feel safe as I tried to sort through my fragmented life.

I am obligated to my family because they are where I draw strength. My wife, despite the pain and hardships it may have caused, stood back and allowed me to set sail on this journey. She shelters me and makes me feel safe when I sleep. This isn't a responsibility she necessarily wanted to accept, but because of her unconditional love, she agreed to be my shelter.

Much like the character in the movie, I am hoping to deliver this message (a figurative package) to a larger audience: it's ok to go through crisis and be lost, but only if you realize you have obligations to yourself and your loved ones that cannot be ignored forever. When I stopped to consider the steps I went through to overcome my tragedy, accept my crisis, listen to my passion and face my regrets as a way of moving forward, I realized that I had an obligation to share this process with others who are still standing on the threshold between the past and the present. I feel Blake would be proud of me for sharing this journey with others so they can know that sometimes heart-wrenching pain is a necessary part of transformation.

This book is my obligation not only to him, but also to the commitments in my life that are larger than my own personal crisis. For my wife who supported me, for Jacob, who was still willing to reach out when I was finally ready, and for all my friends and family who wanted the best for me, this is my way of showing them it wasn't all for nothing. I'm coming off that island now and cannot thank them enough for making me feel safe and loved – sheltered – while I was (emotionally) away.

Surviving a crisis doesn't make a person special, but it gives them a perspective that empowers them to act differently and with passion. By their doing so, perhaps this encourages others to make affirmations about the people they want to be and helps them set goals to get there.

My life is not perfect by any means, and I have much work to do, but I am gaining the tools I need to continue my personal growth and earn back some new measure of normal life my family can depend on. If these words can help you through your own crisis, you will start to see that good deeds are truly met with good results.   After difficult transformation, living well is the best way to honor those who have always been there, doing their best to protect and comfort you even when the weather got a little rough.

11. THE PARALLEL

Throughout the previous chapters, I've talked about foundations, tragedy and crisis, facing regret, adopting affirmations, setting goals and lastly, honoring the things or people in your life that provide you shelter. *What in the world does all this stuff have to do with you, me, and a bunch of birdhouse parts?* Unless your mind works like mine, you might be having a very difficult time drawing any kind of parallel between coping with the loss of a son and building a birdhouse.

Let me explain. In my first year of teaching high school woodshop, I came up with this crazy idea of inviting all the second grade kids to the high school so my students could teach the younger kids how to build birdhouses. When I told my students about this, they actually got pretty excited. The thought of helping a little kid build a birdhouse can soften even the heart of an extremely cool high school student.

We cut all the parts and pieces and had everything pretty much ready to apply glue and nail together when the second graders arrived. Sixty-some kids showed up to the wood shop and my kids and the second graders paired up to build each student a birdhouse. As a first-year teacher, it was rewarding to watch kids who had no idea who I was the year before work with me to achieve a common goal.

The following school year, I received an e-mail from one of our curriculum specialists regarding an opportunity to present at a staff development conference. I had never presented before, so being offered the opportunity made me a little uneasy but willing to try.

I accepted the invitation and started thinking about what I would present. The topic was related to project-based learning, which is hands-on learning. I made a career building projects before becoming a teacher; I learned on each and every one what I would do differently. Teaching woodworking is all about project-based learning, and this is a great area to incorporate the core academic disciplines.

As I planned this presentation, I wondered how I would stand in front of a group of administrators and school personnel who have been in the profession for years and tell them something they don't already know. My only answer to this was that it isn't about what I tell them, it is about how I tell them. In case the previous chapters didn't clue you in, I like to think in metaphors and analogies. Project-based learning should be done with a project that symbolizes the learning, so that is what I set out to do.

The experience of having high school kids teaching elementary school kids how to build a birdhouse had been such a hit, I wondered how effective this delivery tool would be for adults. I thought this would be a perfect time to run with the idea, so for my presentation, each part of the birdhouse represented a part of the planning process that goes into a project-based learning exercise.

During my presentation, the school administration and staff followed along as I handed out each part to them and explained the steps, not only of planning a project-based experience, but also how each part of the birdhouse symbolized that component of planning the lesson. The audience members laid out the parts like they would nail them together (but they didn't), and when I finished speaking the room was full of people with birdhouses sitting in front of them. I received great feedback saying people had really gotten into the process and taken something away from the presentation.

But what has this got to do with me, you and a bunch of birdhouse parts? High school students helping elementary students, a presentation to professional educators – they all got excited about the simple power of a birdhouse. That is when I started to notice the parallel between what people can learn and the symbolism of building a birdhouse.

I sat after school one day looking at a few of the parts that I had left over from my presentation and started thinking about the process of healing I had gone through over the past three and a half years. What about project-based healing? Could it work?

If each piece of the birdhouse is assigned specific symbolism and we put this meaning together to build something new, it can represent more than just walls and a roof. It can represent you and me, and something wonderful that has been born out of crisis; when placed out in the sunlight for the benefit of others, it will allow new life to come from it.

> THE BIRDHOUSE IS A REMINDER OF WHERE WE HAVE BEEN AND WHERE WE ASPIRE TO GO

If we are ready to move through the healing process of whatever crisis we are currently experiencing, this birdhouse can become a symbolic reminder of where we have been and where we aspire to go. So if you are ready, work at your own pace and by your own standards, but begin the process of building something to call your own out of this moment. Turn the page and enter a new chapter of healing and growth, leaving those old chapters behind.

11. THE PROCESS

Like anything we do in life, there is a process. Whether rebuilding an engine or making a glass of chocolate milk, certain steps have to be taken. But we don't all work at the same pace or in the same order; for example, do you pour the milk or the chocolate first? Which way is right? There is no set way to do it as long as you end up with chocolate milk.

The reason I make this point is because the process of building your birdhouse is about you doing it your way so that you get the most out of it. I would be a fool to think that my process is the only way, so what I will do is take you through the process that works and makes sense to me. As you start building your birdhouse and healing your own sense of pain, loss or confusion, use my thoughts to get you started. Each part is going to mean different things to different people. We each find our way out of different crises at different speeds, and there are many different paths to finding the strength to live again. In the end, the only thing that matters is that we end up healing ourselves, so commit yourself to that process, regardless of how different it may look from mine.

The key is moving forward. Time keeps moving, so we need to move with it. One of the most time-honored wake-up calls is "that was then, and this is now." Focusing on the past doesn't make it any easier to move forward, even if we get good at introspection – we need to get living in the now by leaving that past behind.

During my crisis, I attended a session by a well-known grief counselor, Dr. Ivan Smith. His expertise includes telling stories and giving metaphors about the healing process. I like metaphors, so I hoped his visual tools would expand my understanding of the grief process. Dr. Smith told the group that he was going to offer one of us money to drive to a local store to pick up something he had forgotten to bring with him to the presentation. The challenge was he would cover the windshield so that the driver could not see out the front of the vehicle; you had to drive in reverse, using only the rearview mirror.

This represents what happens when we go through something tragic in our lives. The windshield represents our future and the back window represents the past. While sitting in the driver's seat and things are going well, we kick back and cruise through life. Every once in a while we look at the rearview mirror to see where we have been, but for the most part we focus on where we are headed. When tragedy strikes, we feel like time immediately stops and we become fixated on those events behind us, completely neglecting the fact that we are still moving forward into the future.

There is a reason the front windshield spans the whole car and we are only given three tiny mirrors to look behind us. It is important to "reflect" on where we have been in order to understand where we are going, but we can't dwell, or our ability to move forward is seriously impaired. Own the past: know the good times and bad times are responsible for how you have evolved, but also know that at all times, yours is a life in progress.

The process of building a birdhouse is no different. You will work through each part with the past in mind, reflecting on it so you have an understanding of how to move to the next step, and, consequently, closer to the present. Each part becomes a representation of you. I will try to offer direction regarding what it may or may not symbolize. Remember, in order to taste the sweetness, it doesn't matter whether the spoon, milk, or chocolate go into the glass first; you just have to end up with chocolate milk.

On the next page you will see a sketch of the birdhouse parts. This is the perfect time to lay your parts on the table exactly as they appear in the sketch on page 55. Identify each part by writing a small letter in the bottom right corner of each piece. As an example, the foundation piece will be marked with a small letter "F" in the bottom right corner. Likewise, crisis will be "C", regret will be "R", affirmation will be "A", goals will be "G" and shelter will be "S". When you start working on each piece, be sure you are working on the marked side; this building process allows you to express your thoughts, but these thoughts are still personal, so be sure they end up inside the birdhouse until you are ready to share them with someone.

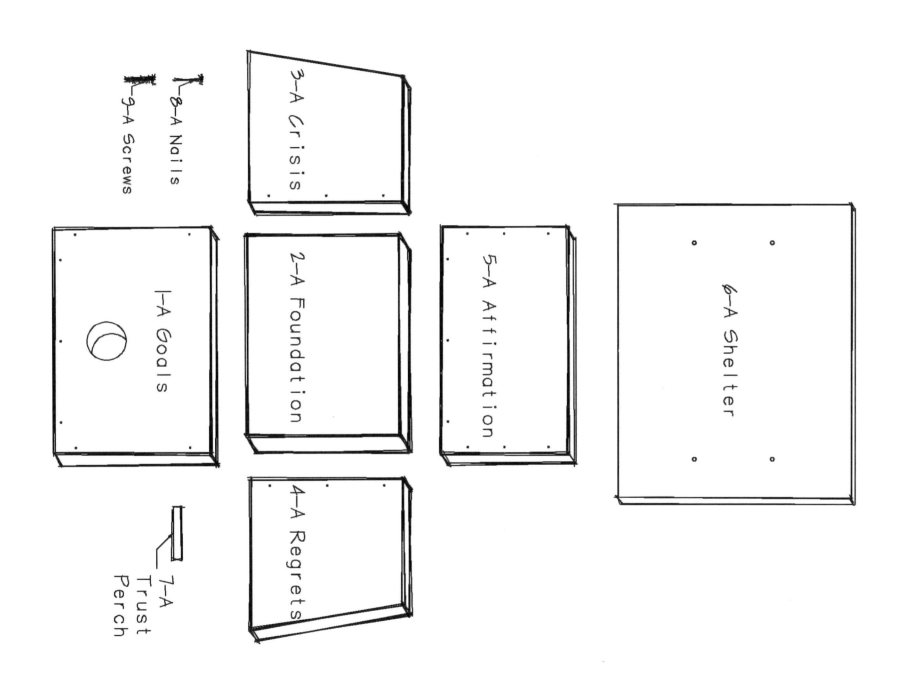

3-A Crisis

8-A Nails

9-A Screws

1-A Goals

2-A Foundation

5-A Affirmation

6-A Shelter

4-A Regrets

7-A
Trust
Perch

13. THE FOUNDATION

I would like to tell you that you can start at the top and work your way down, but it doesn't happen that way. Successful people, ideas and buildings start at the bottom and build their way to the top. I teach my students the importance of having a good foundation for success in life. That is where our healing process (and the construction of our birdhouse) must begin.

The first step in your birdhouse is to acknowledge your foundation. This is represented by the rectangular piece that you marked with an "F" in the corner. It is the thickest piece because it represents strength. According to *Webster's Dictionary*, a "foundation" is defined as "an underlying base or support; especially, the whole substructure of a building." This definition represents what we need to focus on in both a literal and figurative sense.

In construction, a building loses all of its structural integrity, as well as most of its value, if it sits on a weak foundation. If time is not taken to ensure a solid foundation, occupants of the building may experience cracked walls, sloping floors and shifting doors for years, until finally the building threatens complete collapse. Even though the foundation is completely hidden and rarely appreciated, this is the most important part.

Similarly, the first step in rebuilding one's life is to know what personal characteristics, memories and loved ones offer the strongest support. We tend to build our lives on the forces and experiences that blend together to make us who we are. Building a new foundation allows you to select only those forces and experiences that will be strong enough to support the structure of your future; that is the strength this foundation requires.

I know it sounds crazy to think that losing my son offered me some kind of new opportunity, but it did. Once I was willing to reflect on my past to avoid making any more of the same mistakes, I finally realized I was fooling myself to think that my old life still fit. When I was ready to rebuild, I had to know what thoughts, emotions and memories would give me strength and purpose enough to be a part of my foundation.

I also had to learn that dwelling on Blake's death would only cause cracks in my foundation, and I wasn't willing to rebuild under those circumstances. It honestly breaks my heart into tiny little pieces when I think of my son being gone, and sometimes the pieces are so tiny I cannot imagine rebuilding anything, let alone a life without him. But I believe that in order to move forward, I have to build on the strengths that his life gave me.

Here is where you are different from those who have never gone through a life-altering tragedy. They have been building foundations that were made of prescribed amounts of water, sand and cement – everyday events might have caused stress on these people's foundations resulting in cracks or buckling walls, but only real tragedy makes people stop to question the integrity of their foundation. Tragedy leaves you no other option but to rebuild from the broken pieces of the life that once was.

It is your turn to sit down and assess your foundation. Pour yourself a cup of coffee, a glass of tea, or whatever it is you need to be comfortable looking around inside yourself. Take a good, long look at the person you have become and ask yourself how far back that crack in who you are started to show. Some of us need to look a long way into our past and some only need look a short distance, but it is never too late to start healing as long as we are willing to be refreshingly honest about what is causing our lives to fall apart.

Answer these questions:

1. At what point do I feel my life lost solid footing?

2. Was my life on solid ground before my tragedy or do I need to look at an earlier time?

3. Is there any element from my previous foundation that will keep me from moving forward in the rebuilding process?

4. If so, can I let go of my attachment to that and accept that it is no longer a part of who I am trying to become?

5. What characteristics, memories or relationships from my previous foundation will still serve to strengthen my new foundation?

Are you ready to honor these positive elements by acknowledging them on the foundation of your birdhouse?

Sit down with the foundation of your birdhouse; it's the rectangular part marked with an "F" in the bottom right corner. You will always write your thoughts on the side marked with the letter that identifies the piece. This will keep your thoughts inside so that the outside of the birdhouse can be decorated in a way that represents what you would like people to see. If you are having a hard time starting your thoughts, use a fine tip marker and write, "Today I begin my life with a new foundation built upon:" at the top of the piece. Only you know what, who or how much information comes after that colon because we are all different.

In order to complete this step in a way that is meaningful to you, bring your personal touch to this process. If you are a writer, honor the pieces of your new foundation with a poem, word, quote, or whatever strikes your fancy. If you are an artist, you might want to paint or sketch on your foundation something that represents those positive presences that will strengthen and sustain you. If you are a musician, maybe you want to put some lyrics or notes to a favorite melody, and if you are none of these things, maybe you just want to use colored pencils or markers and make a multi-colored list. Whatever fits you best is what you should do, but be clear to yourself, and be honest with yourself. As long as what you do meets those two criteria, there is no wrong way to acknowledge those things that will support you from this point forward.

Being honest and taking it one step at a time are so important; this foundation will act as the jumping off point for the rest of your reflection and growth. Each step after this will move you one step closer to the new you and one step closer to completing the birdhouse, which is a visual representation of who you are committed to being from this day forward.

14. THE CRISIS

Now that the foundation is in place and we know we are on solid ground, the next step to rebuilding is to own our crisis. As I mentioned earlier, I was confused for years after losing Blake. For so long I actually thought that my "life issue," as I sometimes called it, was the horrific tragedy of losing my son, but I was mistaken. Tragedy and crisis are two separate entities. Losing Blake was my tragedy, but not moving on in my life became my crisis.

You now have a strong foundation that is ready to support your new life. Remember, all the details of your personal, reflective, and introspective process stay inside the birdhouse.

While the foundation is laying in front of you with the words facing up, pick up the piece that will represent your crisis. This is the part you marked with a small "C" in the bottom right corner. It is the same width as the foundation, but it is cut at an angle at the top.

A tragedy is nothing more than a disastrous event. It is a significant moment in the timeline of our lives, but it lasts just a moment. You know what I mean if you are still here, reading this right now. My mistake was thinking that this event was what I was fighting. This tragedy was horrific, but it was not my nemesis. The event didn't change you, but your response to that event left you feeling scattered, alone, lost and broken. Your reaction to the event leaves you in crisis, which is exactly what was holding me down after I lost my son.

After I lost Blake, I was thrust into this world of not knowing how to act, what was real, what had meaning in my life or how to feel anything positive. The event of Blake's death was horrible, but it helped my rebuilding process to see that his death was a flash in time; I needed to focus on the all-consuming wildfire I had allowed to be born out of that moment because it was burning out of control. After Blake's death, I felt this disastrous mix of urgency and inaction because I felt his death had somehow become a part of who I was. My identity changed, and I let that happen to me.

After tragedy, we are thrown into a state of crisis likened to driving blindly. We feel ourselves going through the motions, but it feels like a lot of energy and focus without a clear sense of direction or progress. You are all alone on a long road stretching out over a thousand tomorrows where hopelessness and despair become all too familiar. The windshield is foggy, your body is so exhausted that even your eyes fail you, and making out the road ahead is impossible. You try to hit the brakes to buy some time, to rest, to think, to wait for the fog to lift revealing a clearer path, but life doesn't work that way. It keeps moving whether you are in crisis or not. I remember standing at Blake's grave a few days after losing him. His grave sits off a busy main street and across from a convenience store that Blake would frequent. As I stood there trying to pay my respects and make sense of a life now defined by loss, cars kept buzzing by and people kept darting in and out of the convenience store. I remember screaming in my head, "STOP! Can't you see I am suffering?" But the traffic kept right on speaking to me without either of us hearing the other's message: life doesn't stop.

So here you are – choose your metaphor. You are either surrounded by a wildfire you let burn out of control or you are driving blindly – either way, it's your ass on the line and you better start making some decisions. You better stop being scared and take control.

When I stopped to really look at my reaction to Blake's death, I realized that my crisis was the fact that the successful leader I had once been was now afraid to go down the street by himself. Everything I had learned since childhood was thrown out the window and I felt as if I was standing in front of a million people without a thing to say. I could barely guide my own thoughts, let alone the people I loved, and all I knew was that we all desperately wanted out of this.

That loss of control was my crisis. Every business I had opened and every step I had taken over the past several years was done with confidence and a vision of what I expected tomorrow to bring. Once I set my sights on a target, I didn't stop until I succeeded, and that life seemed natural to me. Now I just needed to own this crisis and set my sights on getting through it.

The most important part of taking ownership of my crisis was accepting that no one else was going to fix me. It took a considerable amount of time and a lot of trial and error before I figured this out. I wasn't taking the time to look within because I was too busy looking for someone else to do it for me.

Your source of help is as close as the nearest mirror. It is you and only you. Everyone around you may be in a crisis of their own at the moment, but yours is yours, and the quickest way to turn your life around is to start answering your own questions. Remember earlier when I told Gena I thought Blake was the one who ended up teaching me the most? One of the best lessons Blake taught me was that when crying for help, look in the mirror before you ever look out the window.

Take the left wall of your birdhouse, lay it down with the higher angle to the left and prepare to write on that side. Forget your tragedy – that moment that put your life in turmoil: how do you define the crisis in which this turmoil has left you? Make your crisis into a statement rather than a question. Part of moving forward is leaving these questions behind. Remember though, this birdhouse is about you moving forward; just because I chose to write a statement doesn't mean you have to. You can paint a picture, include notes to a song, or draw something meaningful. We all move forward differently, so be true to yourself and your feelings. (NOTE: Don't write all the way to the bottom edge; for assembly, you'll need to stay up from the bottom about ¾" so it is not covered when you attach it to the foundation.)

One moment can't identify you, so don't focus on your tragedy. We can't change the events. Focus on your unproductive reaction or response to that event – with a little work, our perspective is easier to change than most people realize, and shifting this is what enables us to leave our crisis behind. As soon as I took ownership of my crisis, I started to take control of my life.

15. THE REGRETS

Let's continue the process. You should now have your foundation laying in front of you with the words facing up. To the left side of that foundation is the wall we just completed, and the thoughts on that piece represent your crisis. The next step is to come to terms with our regrets. The regret wall looks identical to the crisis wall in shape, but it will attach to the right side of the foundation. It should be marked with a small "R" in the bottom right corner. Before you begin, stand it next to the foundation with the tallest part of the angle towards you. You will write your thoughts on the side with the small letter "R".

Have you ever noticed how you can have an abundance of energy to do almost anything, and then something comes along and just takes it right out of you? This energy drain is so noticeable that you actually feel it. I can remember many years of building businesses when I could work all day with little energy drain. Of course I was tired, but it did not take a lot to re-energize my system for another hard day. Then I would run across a task that took a lot of mental energy and it would just knock me out. After those tasks, a full night of sleep seemed barely enough to fill my tank again.

Regret is the worst kind of futile mental exercise, and it can have this same toll on you. It can (and will) take over your mind and drain every ounce of energy you have. This empty gas tank makes it a struggle to move forward. I mourn the loss of my son and miss him terribly, and these feelings lead me to be sorry for things I did or didn't do when he was alive. This sorrow is draining, unimaginably unproductive and self-defeating. Regret can zap the energy out of everything.

In the months after my loss, I tapped my foot to a song only to catch myself after a few beats because I realized I was acting the way I did before Blake's death, and even this simple gesture of joy made me feel immensely guilty for allowing myself to act happy. It's almost like your brain is refusing to let you to live again. If the guilt associated with tapping your foot to a song is mentally taxing, imagine how wrecked you feel under other circumstances, such as attending an event you know the person you are grieving would have loved to experience with you.

These kinds of regrets chain us to a past we can't change, and we need to realize it is a self-imposed prison. Unfortunately, there are a thousand different circumstances that can trigger regret.

In an earlier chapter I wrote about walking down the steps after losing Blake only to have Jacob ask for my help hooking his two toy trains together. Even in this most innocent and natural moment, I hesitated to consider whether or not helping Jacob was hurting Blake because of my regret over not doing more for Blake when he was still alive. That horribly irrational thought was like a large, threatening monster, and that evil monster is fueled by regret.

TAKE OWNERSHIP OF YOUR REGRETS

If you'll allow me to mix metaphors one last time, that fuel of regret is as potent as nuclear energy in its power to destroy and leave overwhelming, lasting effects. Think about that: after so long, nuclear fuel (regret) is useless, and yet still incredibly dangerous. We tote it around trying to figure out where we are going to put it and what we are going to do with it. No one wants to help us store it because they know it is toxic. The more you allow the "if only" monster to ravenously feast on regret, the more volatile and isolated you become while carrying around this toxic energy, affecting the relationships you cherish.

I took a huge step in defeating that monster when I stopped to help Jacob hook his toy trains together. There are things I can't undo about the relationship I had with Blake, but by stopping to ensure that the opportunity to spend time with Jacob didn't slip away, I could actually feel that monster of regret get a little weaker for lack of food.

I remember seeing a tattered box of window tint on the back seat of Blake's car after his death. He had been hounding me for weeks to help him jazz up his car just a little bit, but I had made a million excuses. His grades were poor, he had set the wrong priorities, it was too hot, I was too busy – you get the picture. Seeing that sun-bleached, neglected box of unopened window tint almost brought me to my knees. Never, never, never is all I could think, and as I write this now, I vividly relive all of those negative feelings.

But I understand them now.

Why is it so important not only to recognize regret, but to own it? The answer is so we are able to productively and deliberately work our way through today and tomorrow. It is not healthy to dwell on it, but sometimes spent energy is only "spent" because we can't think of creative ways to get more uses out of it. Don't feed the monster; instead, use the fuel of regret to hold yourself accountable. Everybody has regrets, but not everybody takes ownership of these emotions. In their denial, they lose a world of potential motivation to live a more centered, more deliberate life.

It is your turn to face your regrets. If you are like most people, you could fill a thousand sides of the birdhouse with regrets. We may regret many things, but what unchangeable behavior of the past has become your nuclear waste? What is it that zaps the energy from your smile? What makes you feel guilty about something as small as tapping your toe? Is your head running wild with thoughts? My mind is full of them as I sit here writing, but I'm ok. I know I can't change any portion of the life behind me, but I can put them on my birdhouse wall and use them to move forward in a meaningful way. I want them to remind me of mistakes I made in the life I lived before this new life I'm starting right now. Turn this negativity into positive change, one moment at a time. By owning your regrets about the past, you are reminded to never miss another opportunity to do the right thing.

My regrets are simple and powerful, so I work every day to overcome them. I have chosen to write my regrets out, but this is your birdhouse and you can express yours in any fashion you choose. The key is to own them.

16. THE AFFIRMATION

I want to flashback to the previous chapter just long enough to confess that I am relieved that writing about regret is done. As I wrote that chapter, I actually had to stop writing several times because these feelings are the hardest to keep in control. Thinking about writing or facing irreversible mistakes is heart-wrenching and humbling, but it is critical that we find some way to openly acknowledge them.

I hope that you share with me on the website how you have worked past regret in your life. It will be comforting to learn that others have overcome regret and to know that we can give one another strength and support.

In the previous chapter, I said that turning regret into a positive motivating force is difficult, but it can be done. As time starts to heal the pain and you come to understand that life presents opportunities to grow and change, hopefully you will develop a positive outlook. You will find yourself guiltlessly tapping your toe again to a song you like or you'll find that the sound of a lonely ocean crashing on the rocks can bring peace and fond memories rather than sadness.

The whole process is about seeing that the tragedy that occurred in my life – in your life – does not have to define who we are. Take the positive steps to look in the mirror and realize that you control the strength or weakness of the structure you see before you. Look again and figure out just how this tragedy has affected you; what is your crisis? Look into your soul and decide that regret is only a painful, but useless reminder of all the mistakes that are too big to make twice in this one-act play. And once you have convinced yourself that you do not have to be what the forces of guilt and regret want you to be, you will be ready to redefine yourself in very powerful ways.

It is now time for you to set the standard to which you will hold yourself accountable. You need to make a statement of affirmation, committing yourself to becoming the person you want to be. I made many affirmations on my scattered ride during the years following Blake's death. I was jumping from one idea to the next, looking for anything and everything to fix me, but refusing to look in the mirror because I was convinced I wasn't the one who needed to change. I thought someone would come along and change me or the world would change to suit me.

Looking back at some of the thoughts that ran through my head during this period makes me laugh to myself. I almost thought the doorbell would magically ring, and when I answered it there would be a person standing there, ready to save me from myself. When I wasn't waiting on the sound of the doorbell, I was so desperate for change that I applied to be a handyman on a fleet of ships in San Diego. I can't imagine what those poor fellows thought when they received my résumé in the mail. *Here's this guy from Kansas (the farthest point from water in America, by the way) who wants to fix our multi-million dollar ships and he's never even rowed a canoe.* Searching for ourselves always involves unknowingly trying on the role of the fool, and the comedy ends when we realize the answers have always lied within.

I had to turn this craziness around. This quest for some new identity was ruining me and causing unimaginable stress on my wife and stepson, Jacob. Finally, I decided to look in the mirror and make a promise to myself to be a better, more positive me. I needed to set some goals and make some kind of affirmation concerning the type of person this new me was going to be.

In order to gain the trust of those around me again, I worked hard to create a habit of doing what I said and saying what I meant. I accomplished this through starting out small and working my way to bigger things. One of the first things I started was committing to eating better and taking better care of my health.

Yes, my first affirmation was to take care of my health. I looked in the mirror and didn't like what I saw, so I felt the best place to start this process was by simply committing myself to feeling better. It was hard, but it also showed me that starting with the little things first made so much sense. Pretty soon the people around me started to believe that I was steady and dependable, and the resulting boost of confidence showed. To this day, I feel it was that one little step that set my life moving in the right direction.

Let's take a look at our affirmation wall. This rectangular piece acts as the back wall of the birdhouse and is marked with a small "A" in the bottom right corner. As we have on the other walls, express your feelings on the side marked with the "A" so that when it is put together your thoughts will inside the birdhouse.

I put the affirmation on the back wall for two symbolic reasons. The first is because this statement of purpose or identity, what I am calling my affirmation, figuratively "has my back." Imagine that some tough guy in a movie is ready to mix it up with ten other guys – he knows the odds are against him and it might get tough, so he needs to know who is watching his back in case he gets in over his head. When things get tough for me, I want to know that I have something behind me I can trust and believe, and my affirmation offers me just that kind of security.

The second reason for placing my affirmation on the back wall is so I can see it easily when I need strength. Imagine we are building this birdhouse the size of a real house. When you walk in the door at night after a long, trying day, you need to be met with a reminder of what you want to contribute to the world. The structure of the birdhouse lets you see what supports you (the foundation) and a daily reminder of what motivation you have to fulfill your potential (the affirmation). Notice that fears and regrets are still a part of our life, but they are only in our peripheral vision, and they no longer are the focus of our existence. When we walk out of our imaginary birdhouse, we have a clear sense of who we are and where we are coming from, and when we return after a hard day, the affirmation wall at the back of the birdhouse stares us in the face and reminds us what kind of life we want to live.

My affirmation was given to me by a college professor, and his simple words helped me find a meaningful purpose: "People who have experienced tragedy have the ability to do and say great things." This is what I have chosen to believe, and every morning I remind myself of the difference I am trying to make by sharing my story.

Your affirmation may not be words. It may be a person who inspires you, a song that guides your motions, or a picture that gives you strength to overcome the daily setbacks you are sure to encounter. Like all the other parts of this project, it only has to meet your standards of being clear, meaningful and honest.

17. SETTING GOALS

We continue to move through the process, creating the parts of the birdhouse, and, piece-by-piece, we are building a new life. We are symbolically putting our life together in a positive way that gives us direction, and we are getting ready to take our place in this new life. We will put the parts together soon, but for now, we need to remember that healing takes conscious effort and enduring patience.

Inside the front wall of the birdhouse is where you will display your goals. This makes sense if you think back to the previous chapter when we imagined our birdhouse being built to human proportion; in this scenario, the front wall would be the last wall you see when you leave in the morning. Before you exit the safety of your birdhouse, you are reminded of what you are responsible for accomplishing. By forcing yourself to revisit goals related to your personal growth, you are increasing the likelihood that during the everyday, rat-race reality we all live, your decisions and actions arc in linc with thc life you have envisioned and the affirmation you have chosen.

Achieving your goals is a matter of personal accountability. Each person needs to believe in his or her affirmation and find some intrinsic motivation to do the right thing even when no one is looking. This is a healing process and project meant to benefit you, and consequently, the people whose orbits you touch. This is a process of rebuilding, and it is all on you to make your vision come to life. And let me tell you, rebuilding an old dwelling can be a daunting, but rewarding task.

In the past, I was one of those guys who would go look at ten homes for sale and buy the one with urine-stained carpet and nasty wallpaper. I'd never buy the house with nice countertops and bread in the oven. If you are reading this book, then I bet you agree that life is about accepting challenges, conquering them and growing. Earlier we talked about how harboring regret is like carting around barrels of nuclear waste: in the presence of these toxins, we are like condemned property.

I know from experience that if the foundation is solid and the bones are sturdy enough, any old house can be resurrected and blessed with new life, but it's hard when every direction you look, all you see is work that needs to be done. Sound familiar? The key is to look past the harsh realities and start taking baby steps toward your vision of what could be.

Before reaching out to set goals on your birdhouse wall, let's consider the difference between our goals and our affirmation. Goals are very important, but they are not what drive me. My affirmation drives me, which is why I put it on the back wall. I want to see it after a long day's work, when I am tired and most vulnerable to old thoughts and behaviors. By seeing it after a long day, I can do a quick self-assessment to make sure I did my part.

Goals are specific, measureable tasks, which serve as a gauge of how well I am living up my affirmation. For example, my affirmation tells me that, because of my tragedy, I have been empowered to do and say great things to others in similar circumstances. However, a goal related to that might be to get my message out through books, the website and speaking opportunities. If I want to sit down and tally up the number of ways I furthered my progress on that particular goal, I can count phone calls, emails, and time spent writing and editing. After a tragedy, even meeting the smallest goals can seem like huge accomplishments. It is hard for others who have not been through tragedy to understand, but there is no such thing as a small victory when trying to rebuild after being lost in crisis. Hopefully, you are starting to accumulate some of these victories for yourself.

Your goals are going to have to come from your circumstances, just like mine had to come from what I experienced. When I started to get my foundation back under me and started my career as an educator, just surviving the first year of teaching became a goal. Only later, after I had accomplished that goal, did I start to consider how to be a good teacher: baby-steps, people. Baby-steps.

Setting high goals is my nature, but I had to step back from those expectations. I didn't want to risk putting too much pressure on myself or falling back into a slump. You set your goals according to your life plan. Start small, start with one, and follow through. You'll be amazed how quickly sincere efforts snowball once you get the ball rolling.

Let's do this.

Identifying your front wall should be pretty simple. You have marked it with a small "G" at the bottom right corner and it is also has the large hole for the opening and the small hole where the perch will eventually be placed (but don't do that yet). When you have decided how best to express your thoughts, write on the side marked with the "G".

Goals change according to the circumstances in your life. As you start accomplishing what you set your sights on, you will see that your goals become bigger and more challenging. In the beginning, the smallest goal may seem insurmountable. With time and accomplishment, you can "do and say great things." Now it is your turn to put your goals on your wall, as always, in whatever way makes sense to you and the experience in which you find yourself.

18. CREATING SHELTER

The last part of the birdhouse is the roof, but for the purposes of our healing process, it will symbolize shelter. This part of the birdhouse does exactly that: it shelters everything you have worked so hard to accomplish. Ideally, most of this protection is provided to us by our newly realized sense of optimism and confidence – we have, after all, rebuilt on a fine foundation. But we have to admit that in moments of weakness, there are forces larger than ourselves keeping us safe from life's storms.

When I look back the experience of losing Blake, there was a time when I needed complete shelter. My friends and family were providing shelter because I had lost all stability, and I was absently going through the motions. Fortunately, people knew I was struggling, so things I needed just kept magically materializing. When I think about these times, I just gratefully accept that someone was caring for me.

For example, the morning of Blake's funeral I was mentally vacant while getting myself prepared for the events that were about to unfold. As I got out of the shower, Gena walked in the bedroom and laid down the clothes I was to wear. After she walked out, I stood staring at the clothes. I didn't recognize them at all. There, on the bed, lay new shoes, socks, slacks, shirt and a belt. I remember looking at them and wondering where they had come from, because I didn't own dress clothes. Someone had gone shopping and had purchased these new clothes for me. Symbolically, shelter was provided for me at a time when I could not provide it for myself.

When you get your feet back on the ground after tragedy you can start to identify your own shelter. As mentioned earlier, in the movie *Cast Away*, Tom Hanks' character searched for protection and some sense of purpose. In times that seem hopeless, it is good to try to focus on those people who have been there for you. Then, do your best to survive, and commit to returning the favor somewhere down the road; in trying times, it helps to attach some hope to distant tomorrows. If you have lost someone in your life and are reading this story, you know exactly what I mean.

When I was looking for shelter, I started to see my world as being incredibly small. I felt I couldn't do anything for myself, so I think it became a survival instinct to mentally cut off the notion that I was responsible for anyone else. In my darkest days I would have been willing to live in a cave because my world felt so small. What is even more interesting is that I didn't want anyone to provide me shelter. Eventually, I started to come back to the bigger picture and I could see there were people and forces protecting me and making sure I had what I needed to survive until I was awake enough to attach my own sense of urgency to the future.

Little reminders that my world was not (and could not be) as small as it seemed came in seemingly trivial moments, such as helping Jacob hook his trains together. These simple reminders of obligations I had to the larger world started to show up more and more. As I chose to heal and worked on meeting these obligations, my ability to provide shelter started to return, and it happened very naturally.

Something I want to mention here is that creating shelter is just like building a new foundation, understanding your crisis, facing regret, stating your affirmation and seeking your goals. None of these matter unless you are being terribly honest with yourself. Purpose comes when you are finding answers because *you* need them – not because you need someone else to know you have found them. Think about it for a second, half-hearted promises not only set you up for failure, but they leave everyone around you feeling less confident in your decision-making abilities. Do you blame them?

Shelter is tricky because it hovers above you, supposedly protecting you from harsh, stormy conditions, but it is a give and take. For example, when my friends and family stepped up to watch over me, they did so because I had done my part to maintain and sustain those relationships. They felt an obligation to be there when I needed strength I could not muster on my own. Now, at this stage in the process, you are compelled to show them you possess that same strength and, if needed, you could provide shelter for them in their times of need.

You don't do any good by being dishonest about your commitment to live again for the sake of the people who love you. If you are not willing to be honest about those people who helped you through your crisis, glue your birdhouse together any way you want – or better yet, stop right now. Can you hear the tone in my voice? There are people whose lives were disrupted by *your* needs in *your* time of crisis, and if you care for them or believe in this transformative healing process, you will honor your commitment by rebuilding a life that allows you to support them.

Shelter is the largest piece in your birdhouse kit. In reality, it provides protection for the birds. As a symbol of your journey, it represents the size of the challenge you finally face. You must provide shelter for yourself and for those in your life to whom you are committed.

The roof of your birdhouse is marked with the letter "S" in the bottom, right-hand corner. Express your feelings on the side marked with the letter "S".

Before you go any further, take a moment to appreciate the soul-searching work you have done on the pieces in front of you. The process wasn't impossible once you had a goal and took the steps, was it?

Now it's time to build!

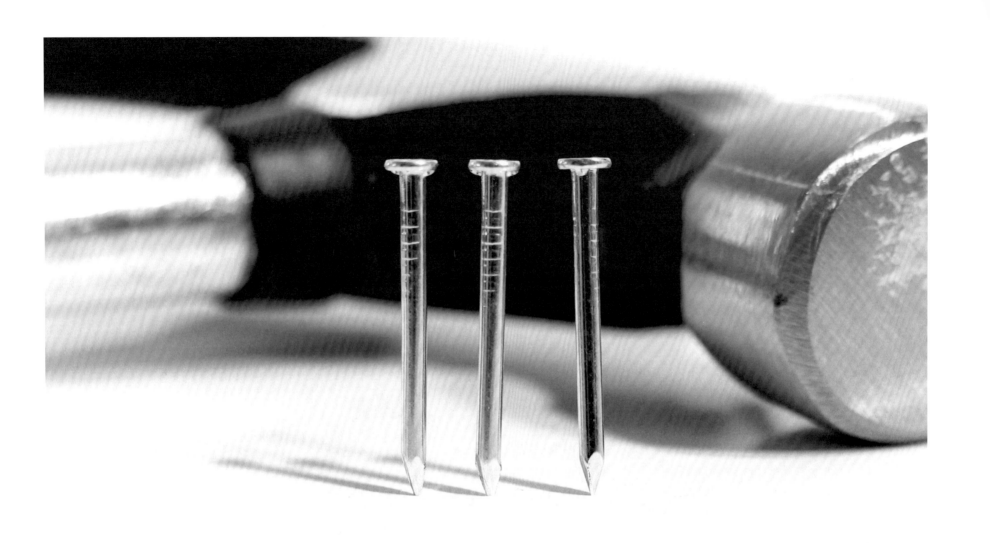

19. PUTTING IT ALL TOGETHER

The title of the book is *The Birdhouse Project*, so let's lighten the mood and have a little fun putting this birdhouse together. This is pretty simple, even for a novice woodworker. The hardest part of this project was digging deep inside yourself, using these tools to claw, poke, prod, split and pound out your emotions, but that part is behind us. All this work of looking at who we are ready to be after enduring loss or crisis will mean nothing if we can't put it all together. The birdhouse acts as a wonderful metaphor for the rebuilding and strengthening process we have undergone.

It is so simple, yet it fits so perfectly in this hands-on healing process. As a birdhouse, its purpose is to be a safe haven for any bird; it is not up to you who moves in. A birdhouse is a foundation, four walls, perch and roof. Yet when assembled, this simple thing can protect life because it provides shelter from sun, wind, rain and predators.

<u>NOTE:</u> YOU WILL NEED:

- FLAT WORK SURFACE
- SMALL BOTTLE OF WOOD GLUE
- HAMMER
- PHILLIPS SCREWDRIVER
- ENCLOSED HARDWARE PACKET
- DAMP PAPER TOWEL

Sometimes the answer is so simple. A perfect example is a windshield wiper. Take a moment to picture this: you are driving along peacefully, when out of the blue you are hit by a violent thunderstorm. There is torrential rain coming from every direction and the wind is almost pushing you off the road. What do you do? You reach for a little switch that makes a flat piece of metal with a rubber strip flip back and forth across the windshield. Thanks to this simple invention, the path you are on becomes clear again and you can successfully navigate what might have otherwise been a destructive, debilitating event. If not for that simple switch, your choices would have been to pull over and wait it out, or forge ahead blindly, inevitably losing control.

This birdhouse is just as simple. We take these pieces and we invest them with meaning. We take each block and use it to assert ownership over the life we feel like we are losing, as well as the one we have yet to find. We take the fragmented pieces of our grief, fears, regrets and relationships and we use our hands, hearts and minds to express our desire to build a new life from the scattered remains.

If I were to lay the unassembled parts of my birdhouse out on my fence, a week from now they would still be there, untouched by any birds searching for a home. I could wait a month before checking again, but there would be no change. Leaving the pieces of a scattered life strewn about for years will never attract anyone except scavengers. But if we just slow down to look at ourselves honestly, if we take the time to inventory what emotions and truths we carried with us out of our crisis, we are forced to pick up the pieces and (for the sake of ourselves and our loved ones) make our lives whole again.

If we place a strong, inviting, fully-assembled birdhouse outside, within days the birds are flying by, landing a few feet away to check it out. Every day they move closer. They see this new structure, this place of strength built on a strong foundation, and they start to trust it is a safe place. They begin to settle in, and soon enough, they feel comfortable and protected in this new place. Just like birds, sooner or later people are going to start flocking to your front door to get a peek inside to see if you might just be the person they were looking for all along – a much more aware you living comfortably in this new normal.

*   *   *

Let's pick up the pieces of our broken lives and build a new future. Let's give the people we love a symbol that we are ready to move forward. Let's show ourselves, our friends and our families that we are back. Let's prove we are ready to be the strength we once needed and invite them to share our sunshine again.

Let's start! (If you are a visual learner, there is a short video segment on how to assemble your birdhouse at **www.thebirdhouseproject.com**).

Please take a few moments to organize your parts like the photo on page 82 to ensure you have what you need. When laying the pieces of wood

out, the sides with your contributions should face up. Please carefully read these pages; you don't want to miss a thing.

We will start with the foundation and left wall (crisis). Place a small bead of glue on the left end of the foundation.

Stand the piece vertically on end and place the straight, pre-drilled edge of the crisis wall on the end of the foundation

as shown (be sure your words or pictures are facing inside the birdhouse). Continue to hold the foundation up vertically

while holding the crisis wall horizontally; this will give you a solid place to nail. Align

everything with the bottom and edges so it is square. Put two of the supplied nails in the

pre-drilled holes and tap them with a hammer to get them started. When it is all lined up, drive the nails in until they

reach the surface. If any excess glue comes out between the pieces, just use the damp paper towel to wipe it up.

Most standard wood glues clean up easily using this method.

Next, set the first part on its side as shown to the photo above and locate your regret wall. After you have

placed a bead of glue on the end of the foundation where the regret wall will go (ensuring that the words

or pictures are to the inside), you will do the same thing you did on the crisis wall. Line the pieces up,

place a couple nails in the pre-drilled holes, and tap them so they are started. When you have the pieces

adjusted like you want them, drive the nails in until they are flush. You should now have a partially

assembled birdhouse that resembles the image to the right.

Isn't this fun? I love building stuff!

With the above portion complete, lay the part on its face, like a horseshoe with the open end toward

you, and pick up your affirmation wall (long, rectangular piece with seven pre-drilled holes). Place a

bead of glue on the edge of the crisis, regret and foundation assembly which will come in contact with

the affirmation wall. Place the affirmation wall (with words to the inside) flat onto your assembled

structure, lining up all of the edges. Place a nail in each side and tap them gently so the boards can

still be lined up. When you think you have it square, drive all seven nails in until they are flush with

the surface. It should look like the picture to the right.

The last wall is the wall that symbolizes our goals. It should be the only wall left and

should have two holes in the middle of it, one large and one small. Lay your birdhouse

on the back wall and apply a small bead of glue to the front edge. The wall

representing my goals has seven pre-drilled holes in it, just like the affirmation wall.

Place the wall with the words inside and the perch hole toward the foundation. Just

like before, insert a couple nails in each side to hold it in place. Line it up and then

drive the rest of the nails down until they are flush.

There is one piece of the birdhouse that has yet to be discussed, and this seems the appropriate time. One of the final parts besides the roof is the perch. This is the small round dowel that was in your packet of nails and screws. This is a brand new reality, and any curious bird wants a place that allows it to get close enough to check it out without actually entering just yet. It needs to look around a bit and build trust before it can commit to living in this new home. Somewhere in the future, after it has moved in and become acclimated to this new reality, that bird will stop using the perch to question the safety and stability of this place, and will instead see it as a beautiful place to sit and gather sunshine.

The perch of trust is very easy to install. Just place a small amount of glue on one end and use your finger to spread the glue around the circumference of that half. Place the glued end in the small opening below the doorway and gently tap it until it is flush on the inside.

The last step in assembly is to attach the roof (we have been calling this our shelter piece). The shelter piece has four holes, and each hole has a tapered side. The tapered side of the holes should face the outside of the birdhouse, allowing the four screws from the hardware package to be driven flush. There are two reasons we are using screws on the roof as opposed to nails: First, I am never going to nail my future shut. The

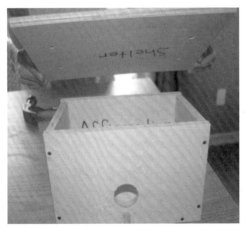

process of rebuilding doesn't end when this birdhouse is complete, and placing nails in the roof closes your birdhouse to future improvements or the ability to revisit your thoughts. This project represents your new life, and maintaining that life comes with the duties of reflection, revision and renewal. Having the shelter piece screwed on allows you to open it up and get a fresh perspective. Secondly, if you place nails in your roof, it is impossible to clean the birdhouse at the beginning of the new season. Just like in our lives, we need to be able to open our birdhouse up and clean out old clutter that is keeping us from hosting new life.

Let's attach your shelter. Set your birdhouse down with the front facing you. **Do not apply glue.** Remember, we want to be able to take it off from time to time. Place the shelter piece on top with the words facing the inside. There are predrilled holes in the top edges so that the screws will go in pretty easily. If the holes do not line up perfectly, the screws will still fit. Insert the four screws provided.

The completed birdhouse will look like the picture on the following page. Well, what do you think? Inside are all your thoughts and dreams of how you will move forward. All that is left is the outside. How do you want people to see you? My birdhouse is just a simple brown; however, I encourage you to listen to your creative impulses. If you plan to put your birdhouse outside (which I highly encourage you to do so you can get the full experience of watching simple pieces of wood come alive by hosting new life), please paint it first. I would put a couple coats of exterior latex paint on to protect the wood. This is a celebration of who you are now, so I encourage honesty and creativity when representing the new you.

Hopefully, when you are done with your birdhouse, you will go to **www.thebirdhouseproject.com** to share your story and a picture of your birdhouse. Why do I think this is important? Sharing your story is important because it creates a support network for those who are healing. Healing alone is like a single cable attempting to hold up an extension bridge; it will not survive that level of strain. However, if we go through these steps individually and then combine our stories, successes and failures create one large support cable, and we can support the weight of anything if we work together.

CONGRATULATIONS! WE WELCOME YOUR STORY.

WWW.THEBIRDHOUSEPROJECT.COM

20. JUSTIFYING THE JOURNEY

You are at the end of this book, but not even close to the end of this journey. Loss is inevitable in this world, and it allows us to dig deeper than we ever imagined. Reading a book about a guy in Kansas who lost his son is truly no different than reading a book about a lady in Pennsylvania who lost her daughter. It's no different than the young man down the street who, after realizing what he had lost in his divorce, decided to write a book about his recovery and changing his life.

I feel a difference in myself by living this process, and that power is what I set out to share with you. Every day, I am learning that my affirmation is true; people who endure tragedy *can* do and say great things, and I don't think for one minute that this is some kind of exclusive, one-man club.

It is up to someone else to decide the worth of these contributions to the people I meet and the commitments I make. After leaving behind a life filled with despair and thoughts of suicide, I am doing what I can to start making my contributions. So far it feels rewarding enough to justify the journey.

I know what worked for me. When my professor spoke those words to me about doing and saying great things, I had more questions than direction. *How do I say great things? What in the world does he mean? Who am I going to convince to sit down and listen to me?* His words left me inspired, but that's not always a direct precursor to action. So here is the greatest lesson I had to learn: sometimes we need to *take action* in order to make sense of feeling lost. You can write all the feelings in the world on a block of wood and assemble them into the grandest structure on earth, but without doing great things for yourself first, you'll never be any good to anyone else.

There is a reason I hear this over and over again, and it is not just because it is a catchy phrase: "Change starts with me." **If you remember nothing else you've read in this book, remember this – believing those four words is *always* the first step.**

You have the tools to make a difference in your life, but sometimes you need to rummage around until you find them. And sadly, until you get yourself together, you are very little help to anyone else. The people we love experience death, divorce, separation, illness and a variety of other tragedies that can lead them into the dark and confusing world of their own personal crises. Those people need you to be there for them, so you need to get back to knowing (and living) your strengths.

Follow these steps to a new you, and do it for the people you love, starting with yourself. My parents watched from the sidelines as I journeyed through the darkness. They were mourning the loss of a grandchild and the loss of their son's will to live. As I sit here looking out the kitchen window at my birdhouse on the fence, I think about the little lives that have decided that is a safe place to be, and I know I am slowly rebuilding trust. This process was just the first step in demonstrating that I can be shelter for those people who helped me get through my own dark times, and keeping their newfound faith in me is one of my daily goals.

There is no quick fix when dealing with grief, but there can be an immediate shift in perspective if we commit ourselves not to focusing on the destruction left in the wake of tragedy, but in the opportunity to (and necessity of) rebuilding our lives.

That's what this book is about, and what it symbolizes for me. By sharing with you the importance of establishing a firm foundation, identifying the limits of your crisis and being honest about the accompanying regrets, maybe you can feel the same "awakening" to life I have experienced. I made an affirmation to turn this experience into opportunity, and I have embraced the personal affirmation to do and say great things in spite of the loss I've suffered.

Hold yourself accountable for the life you know you are capable of creating. Make the choice to gratefully release others from the obligation of offering you shelter, and instead, become the strength you found in others.

CHANGE STARTS WITH YOU

Log on to *www.thebirdhouseproject.com* and tell us your story so others can gain strength from you.

Whether you offer a few pictures, a few sentences or a few pages of pent-up emotions, cast off the

story of loss and re-imagine the life you are ready to host. Together, we can build a network of

thousands of people who are doing and saying great things;

it all begins with you picking up the scattered pieces and putting your life back together again.